TRUE CRIME

Poisoning

John Townsend

Raintree

www.raintreepublishers.co.uk

Visit our website to find out more information about **Raintree** books.

To order:
 Phone 44 (0) 1865 888113

Send a fax to 44 (0) 1865 314091

Visit the Raintree Bookshop at **www.raintreepublishers.co.uk** to browse our catalogue and order online.

First published in Great Britain by
Raintree, Halley Court, Jordan Hill, Oxford OX2 8EJ,
part of Harcourt Education.
Raintree is a registered trademark of Harcourt
Education Ltd.

Editorial: Melanie Copland and Kate Buckingham
Design: Michelle Lisseter and Kamae Design
Picture Research: Maria Joannou and
Ginny Stroud-Lewis
Index: Indexing Specialists (UK) Ltd
Production: Duncan Gilbert

Originated by Dot Gradations Ltd
Printed and bound in China
by South China Printing Company

ISBN 1 844 43590 3
08 07 06 05 04
10 9 8 7 6 5 4 3 2 1

British Library Cataloguing in Publication Data
Townsend, John
Poisoning – (True Crime)
364.1'5
A full catalogue record for this book is available from
the British Library.

Acknowledgements
A–Z botanical p.12; Alamy Images pp. **6–7**
(Goodshot), **8** (John Branscombe), **15** (Howard Rice);
AP/Atusushi Tsukada p. **43**; Art Directors/Trip p. **39**;
Bridgeman p. **9**; Corbis pp. **11, 24, 29** (Bettmann), **22,
27** (Harcourt Index), **40** (M.Mcloughlin/N.Y.POST),
12–13 (Robert Holmes), **28** (Roger Ball), **7** (Roger
Tidman), **4** (Ted Streshinsky), **25** (Tim Wright), **42–43**
(CorbisSygma/Mike Stooke); Hulton Archive pp. **13,
17, 34, 35**; Mary Evans Picture Library p. **16**; PA
Photos p. **37, 8–9** (EPA), **26** (John Giles); Peter
Newark's Pictures pp. **30, 32, 33**; Photodisc/Harcourt
index pp. **10, 14–15**; Popperfoto pp. **23, 21, 36–37**;
Science Photo Library pp. **38–39** (Michael Downe), **38**
(Deep Light Productions), **36** (Jerry Mason), **26, 27,
30** (John Cole); The Kobal Collection pp. **4–5**;
Topham Picturepoint pp. **32, 19, 22, 23**; Trip p.**14**
(H Rogers), **28–29** (R Nichols), **31** (W Watts); Tudor
Photography pp. **10–11, 16–17, 18–19, 20, 24–25, 41**.

Cover photograph of toxic label reproduced with
permission of Getty Images/Brand X

Contents

Any words appearing in the text in bold, like this, are explained in the Glossary. You can also look out for them in the Word Bank at the bottom of each page.

It is usually secret. It is often quiet with no mess. It can be a powder, liquid or gas. The killer does not even have to be there when death strikes. It has been the favourite murder weapon for centuries. It is sometimes tasteless, cannot be seen and works quickly. Just a small six letter word has been many people's last as they choke: POISON!

Before modern science could find tiny **traces** of chemicals in a dead body, many poisoners were never discovered. Death was thought to be due to 'natural causes'. Poison was the ideal tool for murder.

What is poison?

Poison is any substance that harms or kills an **organism**. Some medicines are actually very small **doses** of poison that can kill the disease and make the body better. But the same medicine in a very large dose can harm or kill a person. The poisons mentioned in this book are deadly to humans in just tiny doses, so they are very **toxic**.

A poisonous spider makes a perfect murder weapon!

Word Bank dose   amount or measure of a medicine or drug
organism   living plant or animal

Choose your poison

Poisons are all around us. Many are in our gardens or kitchens. They can kill us if we breathe them in, swallow them, get them on our skin or into our blood. We have known this for thousands of years.

A few drops in a drink, a meal served with deadly mushrooms, a quick jab with a needle or a bedroom that silently fills with gas – they have all done the job.

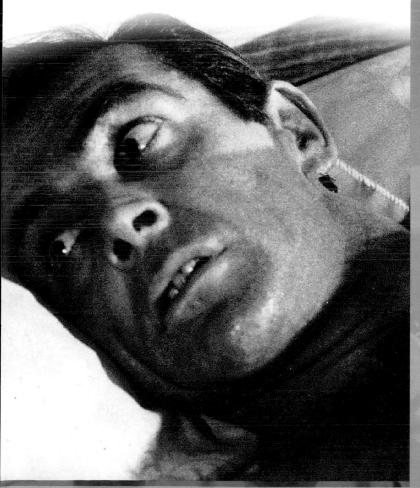

Find out later...

Which poison makes the victim turn blue?

Who poisoned people she owed money to?

Which doctor poisoned his wife?

toxic poisonous
trace very small mark, sign or substance that is left behind

In the beginning

People knew about poisons thousands of years ago. They may have found out about them when they tried eating a new plant or berry. Like many animals, they learned the hard way to avoid certain plants.

Slipping something poisonous into your enemy's food or drink was quite common in Roman times. The emperor Nero had his own poisoner who got rid of people he did not like. Many Roman leaders also had slaves whose job was to taste their food or drink to make sure it was safe. But if it was a slow-acting poison, both slave and master could be dead in a few days.

The Egyptians

Records of Egyptian poisonings date back to about 3000 BC. The Egyptians knew how to make a powerful poison from peach stones. Menes, an Egyptian king, studied poisonous plants. Queen Cleopatra poisoned herself to avoid capture by the Romans. She got hold of a snake whose fangs were full of venom. Its bite was deadly and soon killed her.

Fast Facts

Less than 3 per cent of murders today are due to poisoning.

6   **Word Bank**   hemlock   poisonous plant with small white flowers

Persia

Around 370 BC, the Persians lived in what is now called Iran. Queen Parysatis wanted to kill her daughter-in-law, Statira, so she asked her round for dinner. A roasted bird was placed on the table, with a sharp knife on the plate. One side of the blade had been smeared with **venom**. The Queen made sure she ate the meat cut with the clean side of the knife. Statira ate the meat that had touched the venom. The poison soon did the trick and Statira dropped dead.

Venom from a poisonous snake can kill in seconds.

Ancient Greece

The ancient Greeks used **hemlock** (below) to kill criminals facing the death penalty. The great teacher Socrates was found guilty of teaching young people forbidden ideas. In 402 BC he was forced to drink the poison. His legs felt heavy and his body grew numb. As the poison reached his heart, he died.

venom   poison made by an animal such as a snake

The poisoner's choice

Tell-tale signs

After arsenic is swallowed it soon starts to damage the **digestive system**. This means that arsenic is not broken down by the body, so it can be detected in the victim's hair and fingernails. These can be used as important pieces of **evidence**.

The Greeks knew about this poison as early as 500 BC. It is all around us in small amounts. It is in the soil and water, so we all get tiny **traces** of it inside our bodies.

Arsenic

Until the middle of the 20th century, arsenic was the classic poison used by killers. It could easily be **disguised** in rich food because it is a white powder without a strong taste. It could also be bought from chemists to use in sheep dips or to kill garden pests. Today, however, there are stricter rules which make it much harder to buy.

8   **Word Bank**   pathologist   someone who studies dead bodies

Death

Arsenic does not kill people straight away. Victims can suffer very painful deaths. If they swallow a large spoonful of arsenic, they may feel sick within an hour. Their skin will go cold and clammy and they will start to feel dizzy. Their feet and hands will burn. In a few hours their heart will stop.

Police doctors who examine dead bodies are called **pathologists**. They can spot the signs of arsenic. In a **post-mortem** they can even work out the amount of arsenic inside a victim and when it was given.

Napoleon Bonaparte

Napoleon (below), Emperor of France, died in 1821. He was sure he was being poisoned. Modern tests on his hair show traces of arsenic. But in those days it was common in wallpaper dyes, so everyone showed traces of arsenic. Some scientists think Napoleon was murdered by being given arsenic over several years. But he may have died of a natural illness.

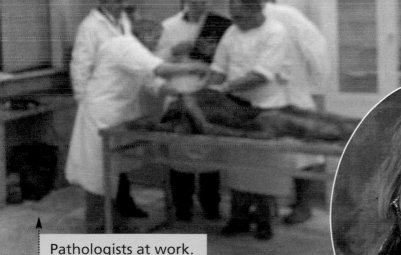

Pathologists at work.

post-mortem   examination of a dead body to find the cause of death

Cyanide

Cyanide is found in many plant seeds. If these are chewed, the poison is released into the stomach and has a deadly effect. Cyanide can be made into powder, salts, liquid or gas.

As a liquid, cyanide can be **absorbed** through the skin. A tiny drop can kill a person. Cyanide salts are used in **pesticides** and metal polishes. One-tenth of a teaspoon is enough to kill someone.

Just the job

Cyanide is the ideal poison for a murder story. As a white powder, it can be put in the sugar bowl. The victim then spoons the deadly poison into their cup. A strong cup of coffee will hide the taste of the cyanide. Within minutes, the victim's body slumps on to the floor.

Poison sprinkled on food could be difficult to detect.

Word Bank   absorb   soak in
almond   kind of nut which is usually good to eat

Fast

Cyanide poisoning is a terrible way to die. It starves the body's cells of **oxygen**. If the poison is swallowed, it will burn the mouth and throat. Cyanide tastes and smells like bitter **almonds**. The smell is often a tell-tale sign of cyanide. In fact, a **pathologist** can usually tell if death is due to cyanide because of the bitter almond smell that stays in the victim's mouth.

Cyanide victims quickly become dizzy and confused. They gasp for breath and may faint. It is a fast-acting poison that tortures as it kills, often within 15 minutes. Sometimes death can happen in as little as 30 seconds.

Just in case

During World War 2, some spies kept a cyanide pill hidden on their bodies or inside a false tooth. The poison was either to kill the enemy or to bite on if they were captured and tortured. It would soon stop them having to give away any secrets.

Hermann Goering was tried as a Nazi war criminal in 1946. He swallowed a cyanide pill to escape punishment.

oxygen   gas in air and water that all animals need to live
pesticide   poison sprayed on the land to kill unwanted insects

Strychnine

Strychnine is a white powder with a bitter taste that is often used in rat poisons. The dog button plant from India has strychnine in its fruit and seeds. Anyone who eats them suffers terrible poisoning. It can take about 20 minutes for victims to die after swallowing strychnine. They often thrash about and suffer from **spasms**. They lose control of their muscles and nervous system. As they die, victims often pull a scary face and their eyes fix in a stare at the point of death.

Rat poison can kill humans too!

Would you believe it?

Strychnine from the dog bush plant (above) first became easily available from chemists in Britain at the start of the 19th century.
In very small doses it was used to help patients feel better after an illness as it gave them an **appetite**. It still has some uses in medicine today.

Word Bank

appetite   feeling hungry
coma   deep sleep caused by injury or drugs

The last breath

A victim of strychnine poisoning does not go into a **coma**. Most victims know they are dying. They experience real terror, then muscle stiffness, twitching of the face and then severe spasms of the whole body. All the muscles go hard and the face and lips turn blue. The victim's lungs fail and they die of choking and lack of air to the body.

Years ago, it was hard for a doctor to detect strychnine poisoning in a body. But with modern science, a **pathologist** can easily find **traces** of strychnine in the liver and kidneys.

Buying poison

Getting hold of strychnine powder was not difficult 100 years ago. A doctor or medical student could easily buy any chemicals they wanted, as long as the sale was recorded in a book. Today there are much stricter rules.

spasm sudden movement of the body that cannot be controlled

Deadly plants

Plants may produce medicines and cures – but they can also be poisonous. Many plants can kill quickly. Deadly plants can be used in many foods – in a salad, a stew or baked in a cake.

Hemlock is common in Europe and America. Its poisonous leaves can easily be made into a deadly salad. Mandrake grows in the Middle East and was used in **witchcraft**. Its roots are **toxic**. Ricin is made from the seeds of the castor bean plant that grows in Africa and India. Ricin is one of the most feared poisons. It is easy to make and a tiny amount can kill an adult.

Deadly nightshade

All parts of this hedgerow plant are poisonous – roots, leaves and berries. At one time, women put drops of it into their eyes to make their pupils **dilate** and look beautiful. Not wise!

Deadly nightshade's true name is 'Belladonna' which means 'beautiful woman'.

Word Bank   dilate   make larger or wider

Death by umbrella

Georgi Markov worked for BBC Radio in London. His programmes upset the government in his home country, Bulgaria.

One day in 1978, Markov was waiting at a bus stop. He noticed a man with an umbrella and suddenly felt a sharp jab in his leg. A tiny poisoned dart had been fired from the man's umbrella. Four days later Markov died. A **post-mortem** showed he had been killed with a tiny pellet of ricin. His killer was thought to be a spy – he has never been caught.

Rhubarb

Many people grow rhubarb (below) in their gardens. The pink stalk is cooked in pies or made into jam. But the leaves of this plant contain oxalic acid which can kill. Although a few people have died from cooking and eating the leaves, it is more likely to happen by accident rather than be used in a murder.

Georgi Markov was poisoned on Waterloo Bridge in London.

witchcraft   using parts of plants to make spells and medicines

Murderers have often used poison to help them out. Some of them have seen it as the only way to find new love, or get rid of old love.

Mystery

We may never know what really happened to Emile L'Angelier (below) in the early hours of March 23 1857. Many books have been written about the case. People still wonder if Emile was killed because a 22-year-old woman's love had run cold.

Madeleine Smith

Nearly 150 years ago, a young Frenchman, Emile L'Angelier, died in agony in Glasgow in the UK. Arsenic burned inside his stomach as he returned home late one night. The next day he died.

His rich girlfriend, Madeleine Smith, had just ended their friendship. She now planned to marry another man. Over the past weeks, Madeleine had gone to a chemist's shop three times. She had bought arsenic, which she told the chemist was for killing rats.

Did Madeleine Smith secretly poison her ex-boyfriend with a hot cup of cocoa?

Word Bank   charged   accused

Arrested

The police found letters from Madeleine in Emile's room. They also found out that she had bought arsenic. She told them the arsenic was to wash with, as it was thought to be good for the skin. But this was not what she had told the chemist! The police thought she had poisoned her ex-boyfriend. She was **charged** with murder and taken to court.

The jury at Madeleine Smith's trial said the case could not be proved so she had to be set free. She later married and moved to London. No one knows what happened to her after that. People are still not sure whether or not she poisoned Emile.

To be on the safe side

Madeleine Smith (below) had signed the Poison Book when she bought arsenic from the chemist. This was a record of all poison sales, that shops had to keep by law. Arsenic at that time was sold with black coal dust in it. This was to keep it from being **confused** with flour, sugar or other white household powders.

confused   mistaken

Death in the family

In 1921, Nannie Hazle married Charley Briggs in the USA. In 1927, two of their four daughters suddenly died with so-called 'food poisoning'. Both children had seemed fine at breakfast. They were dead by midday. Doctors said their deaths were accidental. Charley was not so sure, but he could not prove anything. He ran away and later divorced Nannie.

In 1929, Nannie married Frank Harrelson. They stayed together for sixteen years until she wanted him out of the way. She put arsenic in his whisky, which soon killed him. In 1947, Nannie married Arlie Lanning. He died three years later. She said he was suffering from a fever.

Kansas, 1950

"
Arlie sat down to drink a cup of coffee and eat a bowl of prunes I had prepared for him. Until then, he looked in fine shape. Then, two days later ... dead. I nursed him, but I failed. "

Nannie, at Arlie's funeral. Arlie was Nannie's third husband.

Nannie tried to kill her fifth husband with a prune cake.

Word Bank   confess   admit to doing wrong

Death by prunes

In 1952, Nannie married Richard Morton. Within three months he was dead. Her next husband was Sam Doss but she found him too dull. She gave him a nice **prune** cake laced with arsenic. He got violent pains in his stomach and spent several days in hospital. When he came home, Nannie gave him a cup of coffee – full of arsenic. It soon killed him. Sam's doctor could not believe he had died and told the police what he thought had happened.

Nannie later **confessed** to killing Sam and her other husbands. In 1965, Nannie was sent to prison for life, where she died ten years later.

When Nannie was arrested, all she did was giggle.

prune   dried plum

Getting rid of the competition

Throughout history, people have killed for love. Often, they have killed to get rid of someone who is in the way of love.

Jealous love

Roland Molineux belonged to a gym club in New York. He was **jealous** of men who attracted women. One of these men was Harry Cornish, who soon received a bottle of Bromo-Seltzer salts in the post. These could be added to drinks to make them fizzy and they helped to cure headaches.

In December 1898, Harry's landlady Katherine Adams woke with a headache. Harry gave her the Bromo-Seltzer salts to add to her drink. She said it tasted bitter and suddenly died. There was cyanide in the salts. It was traced to Roland Molineux, who went on trial for murder. But the case could not be proved and he was set free.

Many poisoners have been so jealous that they have added a little something to a drink.

Word Bank

dramatic   exciting, with tension and strong feelings
jealous   resentful of another person

All for love

In 1906, Mabel and Alfred Jones got married in London. In 1924, Mabel fell in love with a Frenchman called Jean-Pierre Vaquier. He was a scientist and sometimes bought strychnine to use in his experiments.

Alfred Jones often woke up with bad headaches and so he used Bromo-Seltzer each morning. But Vaquier added strychnine to his salts and Alfred died in agony. However, **traces** of the poison were left in the bottle. Vaquier was arrested after a chemist remembered selling him strychnine. The trial was very **dramatic**. When the **verdict** was guilty, Vaquier shouted in a great rage. He was hanged in London that year.

Bromo-Seltzer

In 1888, Isaac Emerson made a headache remedy in Baltimore, USA. A spoonful of his salts added to water made a fizzy drink. He called it Bromo-Seltzer. It soon sold in great numbers in blue glass bottles. It was said to bring relief to bad headaches and painful stomachs. It did much more if someone added poison to it!

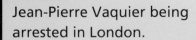

Jean-Pierre Vaquier being arrested in London.

verdict   decision or judgement

All for money

Many people commit a crime for one reason only – to get rich quick. It is the same for some poisoners.

Insurance

An insurance company sells **policies** for cars or houses. Then if property gets damaged, the company pays for the repairs. Many people also **insure** the lives of their family members. Then, if someone in the family dies, the insurance company has to pay out.

Mary Ann Cotton

In 1865, Mary Ann Cotton's first husband died from a sudden stomach problem. Mary Ann was later seen dancing about the house in a new dress. She had bought it with the money from her husband's **life insurance**. She married again but soon her second husband died from stomach problems. People felt very sorry for her.

Mary Ann worked in a hospital like this in England, where she cleaned the wards with soap and arsenic.

Word Bank   life insurance   an agreement that a company pays a sum of money when the insured person dies

The truth unfolds

Mary Ann married again and quickly insured the lives of her new husband, Frederick, and his two sons. In 1871, Frederick died of **gastric** fever. The police began to ask questions. They found out that ten of Mary Ann's children had died. But that was not all. Three husbands, five stepchildren and her mother had all died while living with or near Mary Ann. A lot of insurance money had been paid out after these deaths.

Mary Ann Cotton's trial began in 1873. **Witnesses** told how she used arsenic for scrubbing beds to kill bedbugs. But she also put it in her victims' tea. She was found guilty of poisoning up to 21 people.

Durham Prison is where Mary Ann Cotton was hanged.

witness person present at an event who is able to give evidence

Velma Barfield

In 1984, Velma Barfield (above) was the first woman to be **executed** by **lethal** injection in the USA for 22 years. The execution took place in North Carolina, where only two women had been executed before – in the 1940s. Barfield died by poison, having killed by poison. She had used arsenic to get rid of people she had **swindled** or who she owed money to.

Where there is a will

Richard Brinkley was an English carpenter who met an old lady called Maria Blume in 1907. He wrote her a will, which said she would leave him all her money. He got her to sign it by saying he was collecting names for a trip to the seaside. He also got the **signatures** of two **witnesses** in the same way.

Brinkley then killed Maria by putting cyanide in her drink. Her relatives were puzzled by the will and decided to ask the witnesses about it. Brinkley called on the first witness, giving him a bottle of poisoned beer. Two other people in the house drank it and died. The police arrested Brinkley and he was hanged for poisoning.

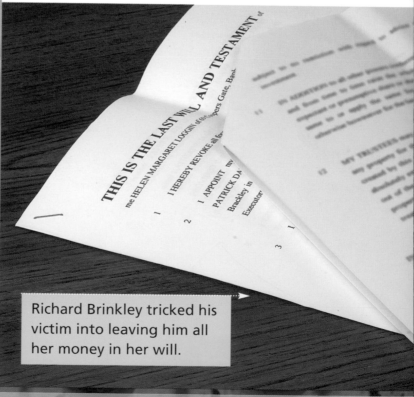

Richard Brinkley tricked his victim into leaving him all her money in her will.

executed   killed as a punishment
forged   false, not real

Arsenic Anna

In 1929, Anna Hahn moved from Germany to Cincinnati, in the USA. She was 23 years old. As soon as she married, she tried to take out a $25,000 **life insurance policy** on her husband. He became ill and was rushed to hospital. He only just survived his mysterious illness.

Anna was a nurse who visited old people. One elderly man died after drinking a mug of beer she had given him. His will said he left everything to Anna but it turned out to be **forged**. It was written in Anna's handwriting. The police became suspicious and they accused Anna of poisoning four men. In 1937, she went on trial and was found guilty.

Death penalty

Anna Hahn was sent to the electric chair (below) kicking and screaming. She admitted she had poisoned four people with arsenic but she did not want to die. Anna Hahn was pronounced dead at 8:13 p.m. on 7 December, 1938. Her body was buried in a cemetery in Columbus, Ohio.

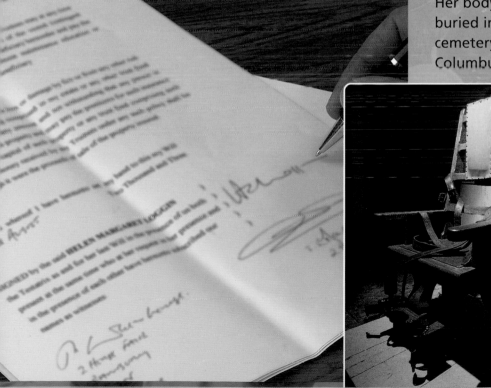

lethal   deadly
swindle   cheat someone out of money or possessions

It is a mystery why some people poison others. They do not kill for love or money. Maybe it is for a sense of power. Sometimes there seems to be no reason why a poisoner strikes.

Donald Harvey

In 1970, 18-year-old Donald Harvey became a hospital worker in Kentucky, USA. One of his jobs was cleaning the wards. Over the following years he poisoned many patients. He put arsenic rat poison in one patient's food. He injected others with cyanide or put it in their orange juice. Over ten years, Harvey murdered at least fifteen patients at another hospital in Ohio. He also stole poisons from the hospital and took them home.

Did you know?

Tiny details at a crime scene (above) are called **forensic evidence**. Often tiny **traces** like grains of poison are found on a **suspect**. Or traces of the poison that killed a victim are found at a suspect's home. This can link a person to the crime and prove they were at the scene.

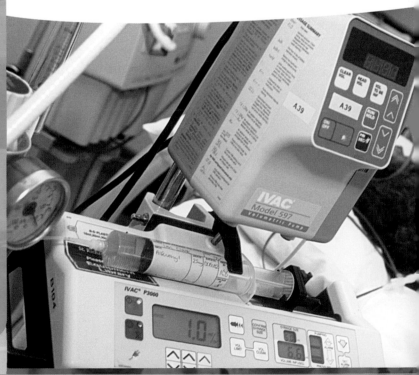

Word Bank

forensic evidence   proof from the study of tiny details found at a crime scene

Serial killer

In 1983, Harvey had a row with his friend's parents so he poisoned their food with arsenic. His friend's father was rushed to hospital. Harvey visited him and put arsenic in his hospital dinner before leaving. The man died later that night.

Harvey murdered another 23 patients that year. He switched off their life-support machines, smothered them or gave injections of arsenic and cyanide. It took time before doctors grew suspicious. In 1987 they called the police. At first, Harvey confessed to committing 33 murders over 17 years. But soon he agreed he had killed nearer 70. He could not say why he had done it.

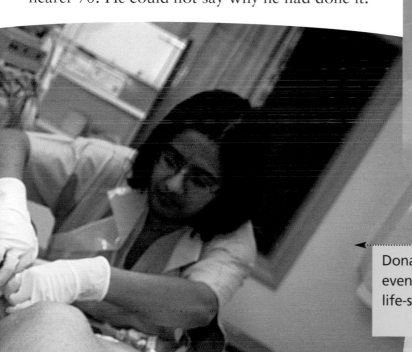

Donald Harvey even turned off life-support machines.

parole   trial release of a prisoner for good behaviour
suspect   person who is thought to be responsible for a crime

A deadly habit

Graham Young was born in London in 1947. As a child he tried to kill his parents, sister and a friend using a poison called **antimony**. At the age of fifteen he was sent to a hospital for mentally ill people. Nine years later he seemed well enough to be released.

Young got a job in a storeroom at a factory. Some of the other workers became ill with a 'bug'. Bob Egle, the storeroom manager, died from an unknown illness. No one knew that Young was slipping poison into cups of tea. Fred Biggs, the manager, died next. When the police arrested Young, his pockets were full of poison. He was sent to prison in 1972, where he died in 1990.

Antimony

Antimony is a silvery-white soft metal that is made into a powder. It is used to make glass, matches and batteries. It has similar effects to arsenic. If the **dose** is repeated over time, this poison can be **fatal**.

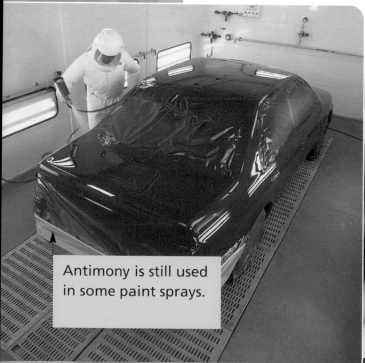

Antimony is still used in some paint sprays.

Word Bank

antimony white powder, similar to arsenic
fatal ending in death

Richard Kuklinski

Richard Kuklinski was a crook in the USA. He stole cars, drugs and guns. He first killed someone in 1949 when he was fourteen years old. Almost 50 years later, he went to prison for another murder.

A man called Gary Smith knew about Kuklinski's crimes. That may have been why Kuklinski gave him a hamburger with a 'little extra' in the ketchup. The two men sat in a hotel room in New Jersey and ate. The cyanide in the ketchup began to work and Smith fell dead. Kuklinski hid the body under the mattress and left.

Cyanide in ketchup killed Gary Smith.

Life sentence

Richard Kuklinski (below) was arrested in 1998 for poisoning a man with cyanide. There may have been other victims. The jury was convinced he was a cruel killer and found him guilty. He went to prison for a **minimum** of 30 years. He will be at least 93 years old when he is released.

Ill people need to trust those who look after them. That is why the following killers were so cruel. They poisoned the weak to make themselves feel strong.

Scary!

Doctors and nurses have been heroes over the ages. They do very important jobs and 99.9 per cent of them are caring and **dedicated** people. But sometimes killers join them. Because they can get hold of drugs and poisons, their job gives them power over the weak. A number have been unable to resist.

Dr Palmer

From 1842 to 1856 Dr William Palmer killed more than ten people in London. After he lost money on horse racing, the people he owed money to began to die. When one victim's family demanded a **post-mortem**, strychnine was found in the body. Dr Palmer was accused of murder, went to court and was found guilty. He was hanged in front of 50,000 cheering people.

The doctor who gambled too much!

Word Bank   cholera   disease causing severe sickness and diarrhoea

Dr Edmond de la Pommerais of France

In 1861, Edmond married a rich lady for her money. He did not love his new wife and he kept a secret girlfriend. But he grew fed up with his girlfriend and she died shortly after he **insured** her life for a lot of money. Doctors thought she died of **cholera** but a post-mortem showed that she had died from a massive dose of the drug **digitalis**. Edmond was arrested. The police were very suspicious because Edmond's mother-in-law had died in a similar way. Edmond was charged with poisoning both women. He was found guilty and sent to the **guillotine** in 1864.

The guillotine

Poisoners and murderers in France had to face the death penalty. They often had their heads chopped off by the dreaded guillotine. The last person to be beheaded by the guillotine in France was Hamida Djandoubi in 1977. France ended the death penalty for murder in 1981.

digitalis   drug made from the digitalis plant

Hanged

In 1863, a fire broke out in a servant girl's room at Dr Edward Pritchard's house in Glasgow, in the UK. The girl was found dead. It seemed she made no attempt to leave her bed during the fire. People wondered if she was already dead when the fire started. Pritchard got the insurance money.

The next year Pritchard's wife Mary became ill, so her mother came to look after her. Before long, she too was sick. Mary died – followed by her mother. Pritchard wrote both death certificates, stating that they died of **gastric** fever. Another doctor became suspicious and a **post-mortem** showed poisoning. Pritchard was arrested and charged with murder.

Public hanging

Dr Edward Pritchard went on trial in July 1865. He was found guilty. He was the last person to be publicly hanged in Glasgow. It was quite a show – with 100,000 people watching.

The house in Glasgow where Dr Pritchard murdered his victims.

Dr Cream

Neill Cream was a Chicago doctor who poisoned at least seven females in North America and England. He became a doctor in 1876. Sixteen years later he was hanged in London at the age of 42.

Dr Cream made and sold pills in his surgery in Chicago. He added an extra **ingredient** for patients he did not like. It was strychnine. When one of his patients died, Cream was arrested and sent to prison for murder. Ten years later he was released. He moved to England, where he killed young women with drinks poisoned with strychnine. One of his friends became suspicious and told the police. Once more Dr Cream was behind bars. But this time it was only until he was hanged.

The black flag

Public hangings in London were stopped in 1868. After that they took place behind prison walls. On 16 November, 1892, a large crowd waited outside Newgate prison. It was where Dr Cream was about to be hanged. When the black flag was raised above the prison wall to show he was dead, the crowds cheered.

THE EXECUTION OF DR NEILL CREAM.

CLOSING SCENES IN THE CAREER OF A GREAT CRIMINAL

Dr Cream's trial was made popular in newspapers of the time.

Poisoning for a new life

Dr Hawley Crippen (below) married Cora in New York and they moved to London around 1900. Cora was an actress but she was not very good. Cora's jewels cost a fortune. She nagged Crippen to earn more money and made him look weak in front of other people. But she soon found he had a secret. He was in love with his secretary, Ethel Le Neve (right).

Cora went mad when she heard of her husband's love for Ethel. She disappeared shortly afterwards.

Dr Crippen told their friends his wife had died. When Ethel started wearing Cora's jewels one friend called the police.

Making history

The famous case of Dr Crippen was the first of its kind. In 1910 radios were still very new. This was the first time Marconi's newly-invented radio machine was used to catch a murderer. The police were told about Crippen by **Morse code**, which used a system of dots and dashes to spell out a message.

hyoscine   poison in the plant deadly nightshade, used in tiny amounts in travel sickness pills

The find

The police called at Dr Crippen's house and found it empty. After searching the house for three days, the police found Cora's cut-up body under the cellar floor. Her remains showed traces of a poison called **hyoscine** – a drug that Crippen kept. Crippen and Ethel were already on a ship to Canada – in **disguise**.

Ethel dressed as a boy and Crippen shaved off his moustache. However, the ship's captain had heard the news and he recognized them. He radioed the police in England. They caught Crippen as he walked off the ship in Canada.

Hanged

Dr Crippen's trial drew huge crowds. One witness said he was a very nice man. But he was found guilty and was hanged. Ethel (left) moved to Canada, taking a note from Crippen with her. It said: 'Death has no terror for me.' She died in 1967, aged 84, still loving her 'little doctor' who had been hanged 57 years earlier.

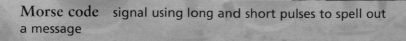

Morse code   signal using long and short pulses to spell out a message

Morphine

Several doctors before and since Crippen have killed their wives. Dr Robert Clements lived on the south coast of England. After his three wives had died mysteriously, Clements married Amy Barnett in 1940. Seven years later, Amy was rushed to hospital in a coma and died the next morning. Clements said she had **leukaemia** and this was recorded as the cause of death. A **post-mortem** showed traces of morphine. The police were suspicious and called on Clements. They found him in a coma and he soon died from a huge overdose. Many bottles of pills and morphine were found in his home.

Painkiller or person-killer?

Morphine has been used as a painkiller for many years. It is made from the **opium** poppy. If too much is swallowed it takes about half an hour for the victim to die. If it is injected, it takes just ten minutes.

Word Bank   opium   drug made from the juice of a special poppy
leukaemia   form of cancer of the bone marrow

Killer nurse

Dorothea Waddingham was a fraud. She pretended to be a nurse and opened a nursing home in Nottingham in 1935. An old lady, Ada Baguley, came to stay on the condition she left her money to Dorothea.

Six days after writing her will, Ada died of what seemed to be a **stroke**. But the doctor was suspicious of a note from Ada: 'My last wish is that my relatives shall not know of my death.' But the note was not written in Ada's handwriting. The doctor called for a post-mortem, which showed Ada had been poisoned with morphine. Dorothea was arrested and found guilty. She was hanged in 1936 at the age of 36.

Doctor death

Dr Harold Shipman (above) worked as a family doctor. He was Britain's worst ever **serial killer** and in 2000 he was convicted of fifteen murders. The police think he may have killed over 200 patients from 1978 to 1998. He injected most of them with morphine. The full details of all his crimes are never likely to be known. He hanged himself in prison in 2004.

Nurse Waddingham and Ronald Sullivan who ran the nursing home together.

stroke   sudden illness caused by a blood clot in the brain

Drug from the rainforest

Curare is a plant from the jungle of South America. It is harmless when eaten but if the **sap** is injected, it kills quickly. The heart and the lungs stop working in an instant. In safe amounts it is used as a drug to relax the body, particularly during lung **surgery**.

Deadly jungle juice

Carl Coppolino and his wife Carmela were New Jersey doctors in the 1960s. After they moved to Florida, Carmela became puzzled. Marjorie Farber, their next door neighbour in New Jersey, moved there as well. Carl told Carmela that he wanted a divorce so he could marry Marjorie. Carmela refused and a few days later she died in her sleep.

Marjorie later told the police Carl had killed his wife. They dug up Carmela's body and found a tiny needle mark in her skin. Scientists found a poison like **curare** in her body. It meant she must have been murdered. Carl Coppolino was sent to prison, but was released in 1979 after twelve years.

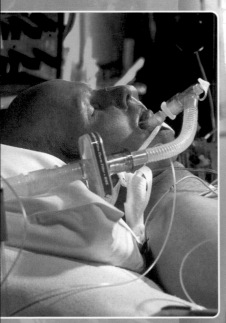

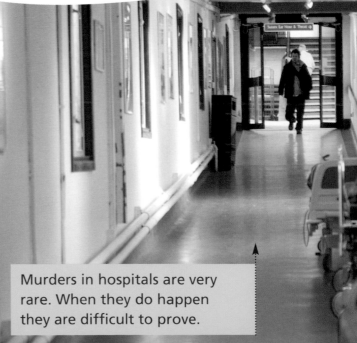

Murders in hospitals are very rare. When they do happen they are difficult to prove.

Word Bank   curare   poisonous plant from the jungle of South America; used in medicine

Murder on the ward

In 1975 up to 40 patients died from breathing failure in a hospital in Michigan in the USA. The **FBI** found that a poisoner was at work, using a drug called Pavulon. This helps to relax the muscles and is made from curare. It has to be handled carefully as too much of it can kill. When not in use, the drug must stay locked away.

Two nurses were on duty each time a patient died. They were both charged with murder but there was no real proof. No one had seen them with any Pavulon. In the end, both nurses were let off and the murders remain unsolved.

Curare

Native South Americans used this poison on the tips of their darts. In 1735 a French explorer called Charles Condamine found out about curare. He said it could 'kill in less than a minute, any animal whose blood it enters'. Some **tribes** call the poison 'woorar' which means 'flying death'.

Malaysian tribesman blowing a poison dart.

tribe   group of families that live closely together, with a chief or leader

Mindless murder

In 1984, Ruth Barrick was a patient at an Ohio hospital. Dr Swango told a nurse he was going to check on her. A few minutes later Ruth was hardly breathing and she soon died. No one realized then that Dr Swango had given her a **lethal** injection. He carried on poisoning his patients for fifteen years.

Other hospital patients suddenly died and some grew very ill. Doctors thought Swango was odd. He once gave some doughnuts to his workmates and they all became very ill. Another friend became ill after Swango gave him a glass of cola. In 1985, Swango was arrested and sent to prison for poisoning.

Poison for pleasure

The most chilling reason some murderers poison people is because they actually enjoy killing. The **serial killer** Dr Michael Swango wrote in his diary that poisoning was 'the only way I have of reminding myself that I'm still alive.'

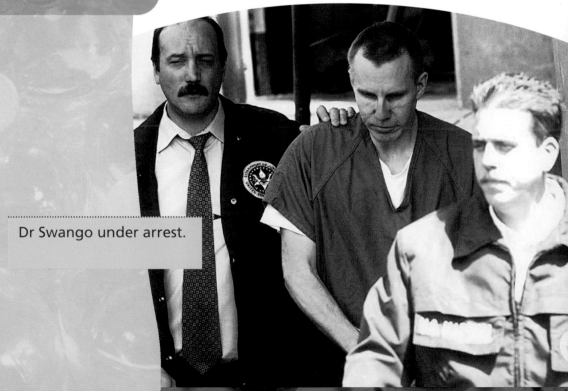

Dr Swango under arrest.

Word Bank   syringe   medical instrument with a needle for giving injections

Confession

In 1987, Swango was released. Within five years he was working as a doctor again, now in South Dakota. He had lied in order to get the job. Some people saw him with a **syringe** just before a patient died. Patients who later recovered said Swango had injected them.

The **FBI** finally began to realize what was happening. By then, Swango had worked in seven hospitals. One was in Africa, where he poisoned at least five patients from 1994 to 1996. In 2000, Swango pleaded guilty to poisoning patients. He was sentenced to life in prison. We may never know just how many people he poisoned.

A sick mind?

What goes on inside the mind of a poisoner? Police found a mass of test tubes, bottles and syringes, like those below, in Swango's home. There were lots of chemicals and he had written out recipes for poisons. Police took away models of handguns and many knives. These were rather strange tools for a doctor of medicine!

New threats

Deadly gas

Mustard gas causes bad blisters, can harm the lungs and even kill. At room temperature, it is a yellow liquid rather than a gas. It got the name mustard gas from the smell, when it was used on soldiers during World War I.

As a murder weapon, poison helps make mysterious detective stories. But it can also bring terror. More people have been killed by poison in the last 100 years than we dare to imagine. During World War 1 and World War 2, **mustard gas** and gas chambers killed millions of people with **toxic** fumes. Today the power of poison to murder millions is still a real threat. Saddam Hussein was blamed for killing thousands of people in Iraq and Iran in 1988. He was thought to have used a poison called **sarin** gas. Taking just a few breaths of this poison can kill a person.

www.usps.com

CRIME SCENE DO NOT CROSS

People investigating poison attacks must wear special outfits to make sure they do not get poisoned.

Word Bank antidote   medicine that will act against a poison
mustard gas   poisonous man-made gas

Sarin

Sarin was developed in 1938 in Germany as a **pesticide**. In the form of a gas or liquid, it has no smell. As a gas, sarin gets into the lungs and the blood, and it stops the heart. It is 26 times more deadly than cyanide gas. In liquid form, one tiny drop on the skin will kill in minutes. Sarin is a serious poison.

The thing about some poisons is that victims can sometimes fight back. Drinking litres of water and vomiting out the poison can be a life-saver. Quick medical treatment and using an **antidote** may stop the poison doing real harm to the body. There is always hope!

Firefighters in Tokyo clear up after the terrorist attack in 1995.

sarin   poisonous gas. Its name comes from the first letters of the names of scientists who made it.

Water

A Chinese shopkeeper was arrested in October 2003 after poisoning a lake. Apparently he thought it would help increase the sales of his bottled water! 9000 families were affected and 42 people needed hospital treatment.

If you want to find out more about the criminal underworld, why not have a look at these books:

Behind the Scenes: Solving a Crime,
Peter Mellet (Heinemann Library, 1999)
Forensic Files: Investigating Murders,
Paul Dowswell (Heinemann Library, 2004)
Forensic Files: Investigating Thefts and Heists,
Alex Woolf (Heinemann Library, 2004)
Just the Facts: Cyber Crime, Neil McIntosh
(Heinemann Library, 2002)

Did you know?

In Australia it is a crime in some states to:

- own a mattress without a mattress licence
- wear pink hot pants after midday on Sundays
- change a light bulb unless you are an electrician!

Criminal records

- The world's first speeding ticket was issued in the UK in 1896 to a man called Walter Arnold. He was travelling at 8 mph in a 2 mph zone.

- The most successful sniffer dog was a Labrador from the USA called Snag. He found 118 different hoards of hidden drugs worth an amazing £580 million!

- The oldest person to be hanged was 82 year old Allan Mair in 1843. He was hanged in the UK sitting down because he was unable to stand.

- The world's largest safe-deposit-box robbery took place in 1976. A group of highly-trained criminals stole more than £22 million worth of goods from a bank in the Middle East.

Snake attack

A man released several deadly puff adder snakes at a bank in South Africa in January 2004. He was angry because the bank had taken his car away. The man was charged with attempted murder after a cleaner was bitten while trying to contain the snakes in the bank's reception area.

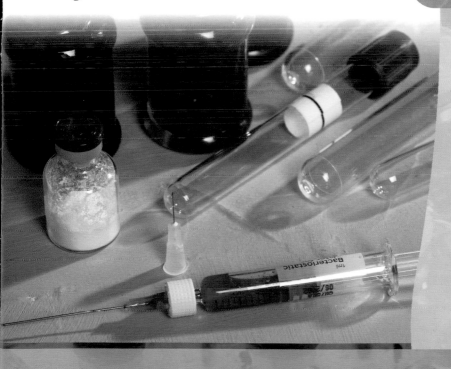

Glossary

absorb soak in

almond kind of nut which is usually good to eat

antidote medicine that will act against a poison

antimony white powder, similar to arsenic

appetite feeling hungry

charged accused

cholera disease causing severe sickness and diarrhoea

coma deep sleep caused by injury or drugs

confess admit to doing wrong

confused mistaken

curare poisonous plant from the jungle of South America, used in medicine

dedicated devoted to a person or job

digestive system where food is broken down and absorbed into the body

digitalis drug made from the digitalis plant

dilate make larger or wider

disguise change of appearance or smell in order to seem different

dose amount or measure of a medicine or drug

dramatic exciting, with tension and strong feelings

evidence proof or information from the scene of a crime

executed killed as a punishment

fatal ending in death

FBI Federal Bureau of Investigation of the USA, which investigates serious crime

forensic evidence proof from the study of tiny details found at a crime scene

forged false, not real

gastric to do with the stomach and intestines

guillotine machine with a heavy blade once used for beheading criminals

hemlock poisonous plant with small white flowers

hyoscine poison in the plant deadly nightshade, used in tiny amounts in travel sickness pills

ingredient part of a mixture or recipe

insure secure the payment of a sum of money in case of loss or death

jealous resentful of another person

lethal deadly

leukaemia form of cancer of the bone marrow

life insurance an agreement that a company pays a sum of money when the insured person dies

minimum the very least

Morse code signal using long and short pulses to spell out a message

mustard gas poisonous man-made gas

opium drug made from the juice of a special poppy

organism living plant or animal

oxygen gas in air and water that all animals need to live

parole trial release of a prisoner for good behaviour

pathologist someone who studies the effects of disease and injury on dead bodies

pesticide poison sprayed on the land to kill unwanted insects

policy contract for insurance

post-mortem examination of a dead body to find the cause of death

prune dried plum

sap juice in the stem or leaves of a plant

sarin poisonous gas. Its name comes from the first letters of the names of scientists who made it.

serial killer someone who murders time and time again

signature person's name in their own writing, showing they approve a document

spasm sudden movement of the body that cannot be controlled

stroke sudden illness caused by a blood clot in the brain

surgery cutting open the body to remove or repair something

suspect person who is thought to be responsible for a crime

swindle cheat someone out of money or possessions

syringe medical instrument with a needle for giving injections

toxic poisonous

trace very small mark, sign or substance that is left behind

tribe group of families that live closely together, with a chief or leader

venom poison made by an animal such as a snake

verdict decision or judgement

witchcraft using parts of plants to make spells and medicines

witness person present at an event who is able to give evidence

Index

Titles in the *True Crime* series include:

Hardback   1 844 43588 1

Hardback   1 844 43589 X

Hardback   1 844 43591 1

Hardback   1 844 43587 3

Hardback   1 844 43590 3

Find out about the other titles in this series on our website www.raintreepublishers.co.uk